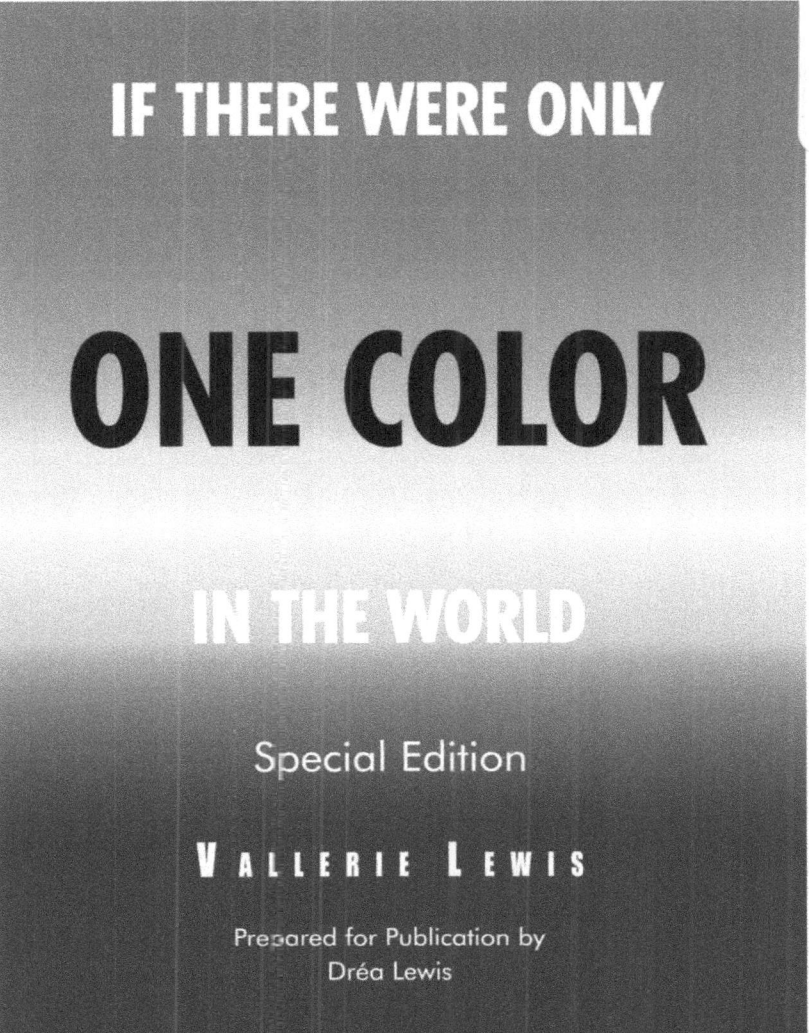

Prepared for publication by Dréa Lewis and

ISBN-13: 978-0692937112   ISBN-10: 0692937110

Copyright © 2017. All rights reserved. No part of this book may be reproduced in any form or by any electronic or mechanical means, including information storage and retrieval systems, without permission in writing from Vallerie Lewis or Dréa Lewis, except by a reviewer, who may quote brief passages in a review.

We welcome your comments and suggestions. Please write to us at:
Dream of Dréa
817 W. Peachtree ST NW
Suite A180-110
Info@DreamOfDrea.com

PREFACE

This book is a collection of poems that originated from memories of family times. I realized the importance of family connection and how family ties can help elevate a person's aspirations. I feel FAMILY is the root to all success.

ACKNOWLEDGEMENTS

Thank you to my family! I am so grateful to my roots, the Lewis, Williams, other family members, and friends, for being there and being a pivotal part of my life to help me to soar. Special thanks to Dream of Dréa for helping me elevate to the next level, and artists Sobia Ashraf and Nonuzza for their designs for illustrations. I feel FAMILY is the root to all success

TABLE OF CONTENTS

If There Were Only One Color In The World

It's So Great To Wear No Socks Or Shoes Today!

Fireflies

Do Plants Sleep At Night?

The Barnyard Animals Frolic

The Black Crows

Lady

The Heart and Soul of Nature

Sweet, Sweet, Mama, Please, Sweet Potato Pie

Babbling Brook

If There Were Only One Color In The World

If there were only one color in the world and that color was yellow,
I know the world would not be mellow.
For rain would began to protest
Because sunny would never rest.
How sad the dew drops would be
That fluffy clouds were gone away permanently.
Even the plants and animals would feel no robust
When cool waters were gone to quench their thirst.
The trees' foliage would be aghast
Because the color green would be a memory of the past.
And air would probably travel a distance
Because Earth would unlikely have none in existence.

If there were only one color in the world and that color was brown,
The ground might have a frown
Because the sparkling waters of shades of blue
Would quickly say adios and ado.
And sadly ground would miss cooling waters' soothing touch.
Consequently, the loose pebbles would sit idle on land's porch.
And the sediments would find themselves stationary
As the time would go from minutes to a century.
Then land might become a solid cement concurrently
As the rolling oceans and seas could become still indefinitely.
Soon the pondering sky would become unsure
As what could be the cure
Since brown stuck around
The Earth's spinning
Figure that revolved in the atmosphere.
Even the other planets would fear
That the pretty colors that used to be near
Are since gone away in Earth's spiraling atmosphere.

If there were only one color in the world and that color was blue,
Glaciers would soon become few.
Eventually polar meltdown would happen so fast.
Then gases would be released from icy masses.
Splashing waters would happily roam
Over every mountain and home.
Soon cool waters would not think it so cool
To exist in this gigantic pool.
Since land and water have always had a plan
To protect the lives of every animal, plant, and man.

But if color blue were to become commonplace,
Land animals and plants would soon have no place.
Alas, underwater plants and animals would miss the sun constantly
And cease to thrive hurriedly.
Also, there would be no light
To guide underwater animals in their flight.
Survival would always be a must
As they would struggle to see their enemies first.
No matter how great it seems
Only the color blue is not too keen.

If there were only one color in the world and that color was white,
That would definitely be a sight.
The icy snow would stiffen
And other things would be missing.
The land would be so barren
As far as the eye could imagine.
Every hill and mountain would miss
How the sun would give a loving kiss
To awaken the treasures of springtime
During the morning, afternoon, or anytime.
Flowers would have no bloom
And animals would not groom
Their sleeping babies never awakened from hibernation.
And soon all of the nation
Would not see the greatest creations
That patiently slept
While white crept
Over everything in its way.
Alas, cold and icy would stay
And would never go away
If the color white decided to stay.

If there were only one color in the world and that color was red,
Heat would always rest its head
On every living thing on this planet
And eliminate most of its inhabitants.
Soon this red planet would not rest
Until it was the very best
In all of our universe.
The flaming hot body would then converse
With Saturn in short verses
That it was the reddest planet in space.
Next the sun would interject and put red planet in its place.

It would be a simple fact there would be two red planets to see
And that's the way it would be.
But red planet would continue to persist
And not settle to be last on the list
As being recognized as one of two
Red planets in outer space's view.

If there were only one color in the world and that color was black,
Darkness would befall over every crack.
Then sleep would roam the countryside
And capture all with droopy eyes.
Then the blackness of Earth would dominate.
And the cold temperatures would be predominating
Over every mountain and hillside.
Soon the beaches would miss the rolling tides
Because the moon would be forced to hide
Its glow due to the shadowing of Earth's space.
Alas, that would end many races
For big and small waves to make their entrances
On beaches whose moonlight was now at a distance.
Moreover the sun would began to see
That planet Earth was as opaque as could be.
And the sun would try with opposition
To brighten Earth of her disposition.

If there were only one color in the world and that color was only one,
Then the purpose of Earth would be few or none.
How unsightly everything would appear
To be seen as a single hue from afar and near.
How the universe would be changed
To see Earth's lovely colors rearranged.
Imagine all those brilliant images diminished
And no more luminosity to be replenished
As Earth revolved around the sun
As day and night would come and be gone.

Our eyes would be held hostage to a lack luster view.
No boldness, no brightness, or spectacular hues,
No candy-colored rainbows cascading into distant inlets,
No blazing horizons and no alluring sunsets,
No dancing colors to awaken spring
No picturesque summer scenes to encourage any jolly bird to sing,
No dreamy autumn splendor to make the world a sight,
And no caressing wintry mix to glisten as the sun shines brightly.

But isn't it great to know
That those spectacular colors have no place to go
And hopes for the future and infinity
Is that those images will always glow in quantity.

It's So Great To Wear No Socks Or Shoes Today!

Barefeet stand, stand, stand.
Barefeet tap, tap, tap.
Barefeet march, march, march.
Barefeet stop, stop, stop.
It's so great to wear no socks or shoes today!

Barefeet twist, twist, twist.
Barefeet stomp, stomp, stomp.
Barefeet dance, dance, dance.
Barefeet freeze, freeze, freeze.
It's so great to wear no socks or shoes today!

Barefeet slide, slide, slide.
Barefeet skip, skip, skip.
Barefeet jump, jump, jump.
Barefeet rest, rest, rest.
I felt great to wear no socks or shoes today!

Fireflies

Fireflies, fireflies,
    Buzzing in the air.

Fireflies, fireflies,
    Flickering in the night.

Fireflies, fireflies,
    Following me home.

Fireflies, fireflies,
    Going quietly away.

Fireflies, fireflies,
    Saying goodnight.

Do Plants Sleep At Night?

Do plants sleep at night
Or stand in the pale moonlight
And count the stars that glimmer in the sky?
Do plants shed a tear
Or laugh when spring is here
And dance when raindrops fall?
Do plants talk to the ground
Or simply stick around
As they extend their roots in any direction they please?
Do plants bask in the sun
Or reach high and have a lot of fun
During summer days that seem to never end?
And do plants languish the day
When their petals fall away
Or do they shrivel and fall asleep during winter's hibernation?

The Barnyard Animals Frolic

On a frigid night in December,
During a year I can't remember.
The moon illuminated the clear vast sky
And the millions of stars were not shy
Because they brilliantly glowed up high.
No heat did I feel on my feet
Which awakened me from my deep sleep.
The barnyard animals on Uncle Joe's farm
Must have become quite alarmed.
I began to hear a stir and their displeasure
As the bitter cold disturbed their leisurely
Nightly slumber and pleasure.
I quickly dressed from head to toe
And gather my strength with a dread and a woe
Because I was left alone and this was my show.
I went to the electrical switch. I clicked it several times and I flinched
As I heard an uproar in a distant pitch.
I was quite amazed as I neared
The farm animals as they behaved quite queer.
I peered through a small open hole
To see the animals closely assembled as a whole.
The next sound I heard was unique
Because it had a pleasing beat.
To start the main attraction
The ducks, chicks, and the horse started the actions.
Quack, quack, cheep, cheep, stomp.
Quack, quack, cheep, cheep, stomp.
Quack, quack, cheep, cheep, stomp.
Then the rooster, the donkey, and the pigs did not hesitate
To keep the crowd captivated.
Cockadoodledoo, Cockadoodledoo, heehaw, heehaw, grunt.
Then Bessie the cow added a zest
As she performed with the pigs with no contest.
Oink, oink, moo, moo, sniff.
Oink, oink, moo, moo, sniff.
Oink, oink, moo, moo, sniff.
Then the goats, dog, cat, the geese, and even a rat
Gave the crowd a rousing climax.
Baa, baa, baa.
Ruff, ruff, ruff.
Shake, shake, shake.
Meow, meow, meow, purr, purr.

Scratch, scratch, squeak, squeak, thump.
Then the geese waddled around in a circle.
When the animals did no more,
I vigorously opened the big red barnyard's door.
The animals were not disturbed a bit.
As I appeared in their midst.
I quickly grabbed a nearby twig
And tapped three times on something big.
The animals' eyes were curious and aglow
As I exclaimed, "Let's repeat your musical show!"
And the barnyard animals frolic
Caused quite delight and was melodic.
Quack, quack, cheep, cheep, stomp.
Quack, quack, cheep, cheep, stomp.
Quack, quack, cheep, cheep, stomp.
Cockadoodledoo, cockadoodledoo, heehaw, heehaw, grunt.
Oink, oink, moo, moo, sniff.
Oink, oink, moo, moo, sniff.
Oink, oink, moo, moo, sniff.
Baa, baa, baa.
Ruff, ruff, ruff.
Shake, shake, shake.
Meow, meow, meow, purr, purr.
Scratch, scratch, squeak, squeak, thump.
Then the geese waddled around in a circle.
Next the animals got quite still
Because the returning warmth removed the chill.
I quietly exited the scene
Because all animals seemed peaceful and serene.
Then I was startled from my tranquil state.
It was my alarm clock helping me to awake.
I couldn't believe it was just a dream
And none of the events had happened as it seemed.

The Black Crows

A cool blustery breeze rattled
And almost concurrently shattered
A white pane of glass whose wood frame was tattered.
Then the wind extended its reach
And grabbed clusters of peach
And reddish colored leaves.
With a big whooing sound
It twirled the leaves up and around
The big ol' sycamore tree near my house.
As the gusty wind blew
It obstructed my view
And scattered the leaves everywhere.
When I brushed back my hair,
I became quite aware
Of approaching specks way up the sky.
For in the distance it was clear
Twenty-four pairs of wings would veer
For a space nearby.
With a caw, caw, caw,
I saw extended wings and claws
Began to rest on the black telephone lines above me.
I thought it not unusual
And certainly not possible
For them to rest a spell.
Then without warning
A strange sound began blaring
And upset the stillness of the nearby forest.
I quickly turned in hopes to see
What that could possibly be.
Then Papa walked past me
And began racking energetically
To remove the massive pile of leaves on the ground.
As days flew by, I ended each passing day
In almost the same way
By staring long periods of time out my window.
I couldn't understand
Why more birds wouldn't land
Each and every day on the black telephone line above me.
Soon fewer days did I see
Massive piles of leaves below the tree
That captivated me as I played so happily.
And the thick forest that was a mere short distance

Seemed to change in but an instant
And the frigid wind gusts blew without a hindrance.
Soon the loud booming sound
And the vibrations that shook the ground
Diminished and faded away.
Then the next thing I viewed
Were all the black crows as they flew
In the horizon one cold wintry day.
For a few days I would stare
Out my window with a pondering glare
Asking why the birds flew away on that fateful day.

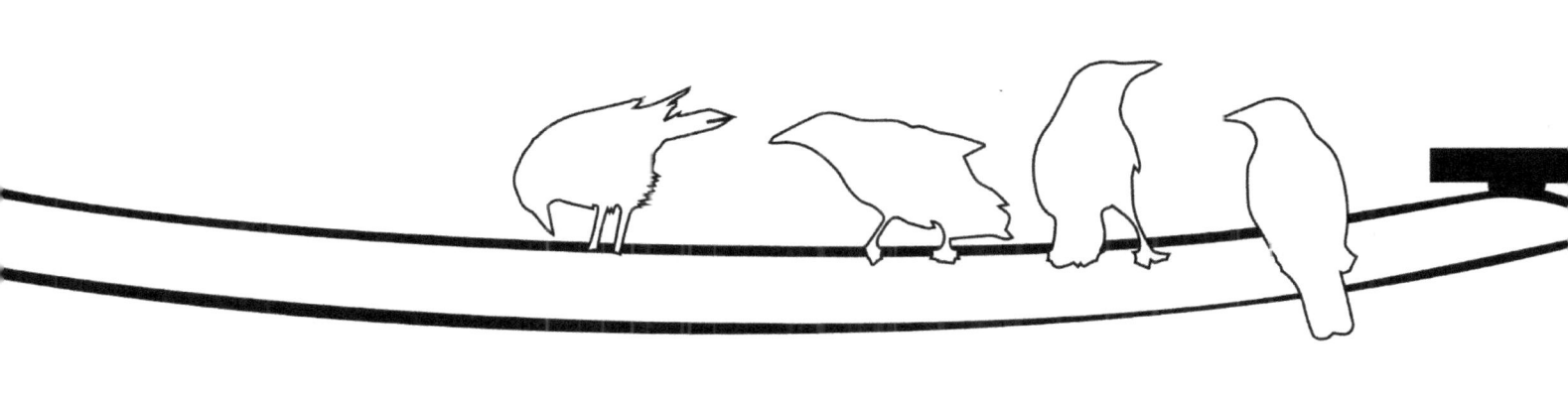

Lady

Through my eyes I saw her
And my heart would flutter and stir
Because she always was so playful and energetic.
Through my ears I would listen
As she ran and greeted me with all her loving intentions
Especially when she sensed I was really sad.
Through my hands I would feel
A warm body and kindred spirit so real
That it elated me in every way.
Through the sound of my voice
She would come quickly and rejoice
As we merrily played in our favorite spot.
Through my heart I felt sadness
Because her departure was sheer madness
When I found her lifeless body beside the dirt road.
But I guarantee
My pup, Lady, will live through me
Forever as long as I will be able to remember.

The Heart and Soul of Nature

Birds chirping merrily.
Bees buzzing passionately
And flowers being pollinated and growing each day.
I think that is the heart and soul of nature.

The sun brightly shining on any given day.
Stormy clouds releasing rain gently to the ground
And rivers and streams flowing easily in a steady pace.
This could be the heart and soul of nature.

Animals storing food in safe places.
Leaves slowly falling from multiple trees
And the Earth slowly moving away from the sun.
Perhaps that is the heart and soul of nature.

Animals hibernating for a spell.
Some trees being bare and not blooming all year
And snow blanketing mountains and other places.
I really hope this is the heart and soul of nature.

Sweet, Sweet, Mama, Please, Sweet Potato Pie

Sweet savory caramelized toppings
Deep, so deep crust
That crumbled as the knife pierced the center of the pie
And glided to the top section of the pan.
Cooled, yet still slightly warmed for the
Hungry children that anxiously waited for it.
Mama gave each one a slice of pie
And they shouted harmoniously
for the whole world to hear , "Sweet, sweet, Mama, please, sweet potato pie!"
Smacking and ahhh sounds filled the kitchen on any given Sunday after church
As the taste of the pie swirled in their mouths
And all took flight in the clouds as the indulgence
Landed home in gleeful tummies.
Soon not a mumbling word was heard
As the last bite was consumed and
All landed in comfy cozy places in a house so familiar to the family.
The last thing was heard was a faint whisper from all while preparing
To take a snooze, "Sweet, sweet, Mama, please, sweet potato pie."
The next Sunday after church was memorable
As several piercing eyes attacked the kitchen
from the window sill outdoors.
With footsteps going hither and yonder
Then the sounds of eggs cracking and
Mama whipping her home-made mixture
As a slight, sweet fragrance started to emerge.
Next the sound of sheer delight
As her oven door screeched opened and closed.
Tick, tock, tick, tock, tick, tock, ding. There it is!
The oven door cried out when it was opened and
The whiff of sweetness overtook us.
Lastly, the silence was disturbed
With everyone cheering, "Sweet, sweet, Mama, please, sweet potato pie!"
Soon the dinner hour arrived
And all plates were as cleaned as a well swept floor
With very little traces of the main course.
Mama gushed with laughter
And moved over to her special platter where the sweet potato pie lay
On her sweetness table.
The masses with plates in hand were bees buzzing around a hive
They glared hungrily as Mama carefully sliced that pie and served it.
The children sucked in their slice like a vacuum cleaner.
And mama said bewildered, "One more piece of pie left?"

Before others could respond, two left the pack like charging bulls.
Each one grabbed the plate and the pie slice took flight.
Then all eyes were watching with dismay as that piece of pie fell on the floor.
Soon all chimed in with disillusion, "Sweet, sweet, Mama, please, no more sweet potato pie?"

Babbling Brook

Babbling brook beguiled a bumbling bush and brushed its way to freedom on a balmy summer's day.

Babbling brook bubbled and bustled its way past bony bare feet and beat a backwoods' bumpy bed.

Babbling brook built a small burrow and beckoned bony bare feet to join the bash.

www.ingramcontent.com/pod-product-compliance
Lightning Source LLC
Chambersburg PA
CBHW081353040426
42450CB00016B/3419